AANANDAM

AN ACT OF COMMUNITY SERVICE

AUTHOR

Dr. Shuchi Sharma, IAS (retd)

Former Secretary Higher, Technical & Sanskrit Education,
Government of Rajasthan

REVIEWER

Shri Anil Swarup, IAS (retd)

Former Secretary School Education,
Government of India

KHANNA BOOK PUBLISHING CO. (P) Ltd.
4C/4344, Ansari Road, Darya Ganj,
New Delhi, India

All India Council for Technical Education
Nelson Mandela Marg, Vasant Kunj,
New Delhi, India

ISBN: 978-93-5538-248-1

Book Code: DIP467EN

Aananadam: An Act Of Community Service

by Dr. Shuchi Sharma

First Edition: 2026

Originally Published by:

All India Council for Technical Education, Ministry of Education, GOI

Exclusively Published & Distributed by:

Khanna Book Publishing Co. (P) Ltd.
4C/4344, Ansari Road, Daryaganj,
New Delhi (INDIA)

Visit us at: **www.khannabooks.com**
Write us at: **contact@khannabooks.com**

To view complete list of books, Please scan the QR Code:

KPH

Printed in Bharat.

प्रो. टी. जी. सीताराम
अध्यक्ष
Prof. T. G. Sitharam
Chairman

सत्यमेव जयते

आज़ादी का अमृत महोत्सव

अखिल भारतीय तकनीकी शिक्षा परिषद्
(भारत सरकार का एक सांविधिक निकाय)
(शिक्षा मंत्रालय, भारत सरकार)
नेल्सन मंडेला मार्ग, वसंत कुंज, नई दिल्ली–110070
दूरभाष : 011–26131498
ई–मेल : chairman@aicte-india.org

ALL INDIA COUNCIL FOR TECHNICAL EDUCATION
(A STATUTORY BODY OF THE GOVT. OF INDIA)
(Ministry of Education, Govt. of India)
Nelson Mandela Marg, Vasant Kunj, New Delhi-110070
Phone : 011-26131498
E-mail : chairman@aicte-india.org

FOREWORD

Engineers are the backbone of any modern society. They are the ones responsible for the marvels as well as the improved quality of life across the world. Engineers have driven humanity towards greater heights in a more evolved and unprecedented manner.

The All India Council for Technical Education (AICTE), have spared no efforts towards the strengthening of the technical education in the country. AICTE is always committed towards promoting quality Technical Education to make India a modern developed nation emphasizing on the overall welfare of mankind.

An array of initiatives has been taken by AICTE in last decade which have been accelerated now by the National Education Policy (NEP) 2020. The implementation of NEP under the visionary leadership of Hon'ble Prime Minister of India envisages the provision for education in regional languages to all, thereby ensuring that every graduate becomes competent enough and is in a position to contribute towards the national growth and development through innovation & entrepreneurship.

One of the spheres where AICTE had been relentlessly working since past couple of years is providing high quality original technical contents at Under Graduate & Diploma level prepared and translated by eminent educators in various Indian languages to its aspirants. For students pursuing 2nd year of their Engineering education, AICTE has identified 87 books, which shall be translated into 12 Indian languages - Hindi, Tamil, Gujarati, Odia, Bengali, Kannada, Urdu, Punjabi, Telugu, Marathi, Assamese & Malayalam. In addition to the English medium, books in different Indian Languages are going to support the students to understand the concepts in their respective mother tongue.

On behalf of AICTE, I express sincere gratitude to all distinguished authors, reviewers and translators from the renowned institutions of high repute for their admirable contribution in a record span of time.

AICTE is confident that these outcomes based original contents shall help aspirants to master the subject with comprehension and greater ease.

(Prof. T. G. Sitharam)

ACKNOWLEDGEMENT

The author is grateful to the authorities of AICTE, particularly Prof. T. G. Sitharam, Chairman; Prof. M. P. Poonia, Vice-Chairman; Prof. Rajive Kumar, Member-Secretary and Dr Amit Kumar Srivastava, Director, Faculty Development Cell for their planning to publish the book on "Aanandam" - An Act of Community Service. I sincerely acknowledge the valuable contributions of the reviewer of the book Shri. Anil Swarup (Founder Chairman Nexus of Good); Former Secretary School Education (2016-2018) & Coal (2014-2016) Govt. of India. Author of "Ethical Dilemmas of a Civil Servant", "Not Just a Civil Servant" and "No More a Civil Servant".

Acknowledgements are due to AICTE members, experts and authors who shared their views to further develop the holistic education in our country. I am grateful to the contributors and different workers in this field whose published books, review articles, papers, photographs, footnotes, references and other valuable information helped me at the time of writing the book.

This book is a consequence of a series of the deliberations held with the Vice Chancellors of the universities in Rajasthan, academicians and the group of NGOs led by Mrs Neelima Khaitan (CSR & Social Sector Advisor) for formalising the concept of Aanandam as a subject. My heartiest thanks to Lt. Gen. (Dr.) MD Venkatesh, Vice Chancellor Manipal Academy of Higher Education for sharing their experience in volunteering in the form of a chapter written by Dr. Anup Naha (Associate Professor MAHE) in this book. I am also thankful for the contributions of Khaitan Government Polytechnic college, Government College Bundi, Shri Keshvanand Institute of Technology and Apex University who have shared their community service project reports for the book.

My deep gratitude is due to my parents, family and friends for their whole hearted support in writing the book. Lastly in all humility I have to submit that the conception of the idea of Aanandam and its translation into the form of this book is an outcome of the divine grace of the Almighty.

Dr. Shuchi Sharma

PREFACE

The book titled Aanandam an Act of Community Service is an outcome of a long thought process that started since I was a student. My experience as a parent and administrator further compelled me to think about some fundamental shortcoming in our education system. When I got the opportunity to serve as Secretary of Higher Technical & Sanskrit Education Department in Government of Rajasthan I took an initiative to introduce a new subject in the name „Aanandam" with a sole aim of making education holistic. The purpose of writing this book is to expose the faculty and the students to the idea of meaningful education, the education which is not limited to text books, rather beyond textbooks. Keeping in mind this purpose I"ve tried to explore the real meaning of education and its role in making the student a socially responsible individual. As this is a new concept it was a big challenge to concretize it in the shape of a subject as a part of the curriculum of education. There had been various attempts before also, NSS is one example which emphasizes on community service. But it's a voluntary activity which is taken up by a small number of the students. Aanandam is beyond that. It stimulates the inner world of the student to bring out the goodness hidden inside. While writing the book on this new subject, I have endeavoured to make it acceptable to the faculty and the students. It was necessary that the chapters are written in a way that makes it easy for the faculty and students to grasp and embrace the concept of Aanandam. The two important parts of the subject - Aanandam Diary and Community Service project have been dealt at conceptual as well as implementational level. How to do a community service project and how to write the project report have been explained with real life examples. Rajasthan experience has been added as the appendix in the book. Based on the experience in the educational institutes of Rajasthan I am quite confident and hopeful that the students as well as faculty will be enthusiastic to welcome this new subject which would provide them an opportunity to enter into a world of creativity and happiness.

Dr. Shuchi Sharma

Syllabus of Aanandam - An Act of Community Service

NEP 2020 (11.8) states that... "value-based education will include the development of humanistic, ethical, Constitutional, and universal human values of truth (Satya), righteous conduct (dharma), peace (shanti), love (prem), nonviolence (ahimsa), scientific temper, citizenship values, and also life-skills; lessons in seva/service and participation in community service programs will be considered an integral part of a holistic education".

Aanandam aims at evolving a young student into a socially responsible and happy citizen. Of course, it is clearly understood that for these efforts to be meaningful, the basic understanding and feeling has to be there. Therefore, the pre-requisite course has been kept as UHV-II: Understanding Harmony and Ethical Human Conduct.

Prerequisite: UHV-II: Understanding harmony and Ethical Human Conduct

Desirable: UHV-IV: Vision for Humane Society

Course Objectives

1. To help the student to relate to the community of people around them and sharpen their feeling of empathy toward them
2. To tap the student"s hidden leadership and creative potential for addressing the day-to- day issues faced by the community leading to greater harmony in the community
3. To help the student refer to their Natural Acceptance in problem-solving

Course Methodology

The methodology of this course is learning-by-doing. The student is expected to be involved in a one-semester long group community-service project and keep a record in his/her daily Aanandam Diary. Each week, a faculty mentor will guide each group of students on their group community-service project and provide observations on the diary entries made by the students.

Course Contents

Aanandam course has two major components: -

1. Daily Diary of Aanandam.
2. Group Project of community service.

1. Daily Diary of Aanandam

Each student will have to do, observe and record an act of goodness in the Diary of Aanandam every day. Any act which reflects caring, sharing, helping attitude of the students will be recorded by the students in the Aanandam Diary. Any act of kindness to humanity, environment or animal world will be recorded daily in the Diary.

There will be a period of Aanandam daily in the colleges. As Aanandam is a subject which does not require any specialisation, every faculty in the institute can be a mentor of students Aanandam. The period of Aanandam can be an extended period of any subject.

The students will discuss the act recorded in the Diary in the class of Aanandam with the mentor faculty. The mentor will tick the names of the students who have done this task of recording a good deed done by them.

The Diary writing is a mandatory activity to qualify for evaluation in Aanandam.

2. Group Project of Community Service

The students will have to do a group project of Community Service. The size of the group depends upon the kind of the project taken up by the students.

Subjects for the projects can be related to all kinds of Community Services related to environment protection, energy conservation, water conservation, women empowerment, literacy, child nutrition, health, hygiene and sanitation, cleanliness of the institute premises, disaster management, heritage restoration, developing indigenous local technologies etc. The duration of the project is one semester.

The group project will be based totally on field activities. The mentor of the project will be a faculty who will act as facilitator and help the students in providing necessary assistance like liaisoning with the Government Agencies, good NGOs, Corporates and the like.

The project report will be submitted with photographs and news clippings of the field work done by the students. A Project evaluation committee will be formed to evaluate the projects done by the students. The evaluation of the project will be done in terms of marks or credits which will be an essential part of the student's report card.

COURSE OUTCOMES

1. Aanandam Course has been devised in consonance with the motto of the ancient education system – 'Ya Vidya Sa Vimuktaye' i.e. the main purpose of education is liberation. Aanandam will let the students introspect the goodness hidden inside them.
2. In Diary of Aanandam, the students will be writing a good deed done by them daily. This will generate happiness of giving.
3. The students by taking up projects of Community Service and interacting with the community will try to identify and understand the problems of the community. This will enhance their emotional interdependence quotient and empathetic attitude.
4. While coming across the community problems the students will try to find out the solutions. This act will tap the creative and imaginative faculties of the students. While trying to solve the problems of the community they will make the community happy and in turn they will get satisfaction and happiness.
5. The students will be more oriented towards being job providers instead of being job seekers.
6. They will realise the key of happiness is not in acquiring more and more but it is in giving and sharing.

CONTENTS

Chapter 1

Why Aanandam?

Our education system is focussing on the external and material world only whereas the source of happiness lies within. Aanandam is a holistic course that emphasises the development of the innate soft qualities of a student to make a better world. In reality, there is limited learning from the textbooks, a student learns the most while doing and when they apply their learning to real-life situations and share it with the people around, then only they understand the problem, this is real education.

Aanandam provides the students an opportunity for interaction of

- Self with Self
- Self with Nature
- Self with Community

Aanandam has been modelled to tap the inner world and holistically link life with education. All the discoveries and inventions happen only when a person gets deeply involved with a problem, Aanandam gives that opportunity to the students. It is certainly going to be a source of creativity and innovations. In the group projects of Aanandam by interacting with the community or by getting involved with any problem a lot of churning happens in the mind. The student while understanding the problem will apply his or her whole learning and information gathered from the surrounding. This way the student will be using the learning for making lives better. Such a process will also help in the spiritual development of the students.

Many of us have heard about Ubuntu - the essence of being human. Ubuntu is based on the fact that we cannot exist in isolation, we are not mere individuals rather we are all interconnected and our actions affect the whole world. Aanandam has been introduced with this basic understanding of a human being to make our human society healthier and happier.

The world has already faced two world wars that resulted in the utter destruction of humanity and t we are apprehensive of such wars even today. Education can be used as a platform to make people more loving, more friendly, kinder, and more human. Aanandam has been introduced for this purpose. Happiness does not lie in acquiring rather it is in sharing with people around us. There is a Bahai saying - "When a thought of war comes, oppose it by a stronger thought of peace. A thought of hatred must be destroyed by a more powerful thought of love. Thoughts of war bring the destruction of all harmony, well-being, restfulness, and contentment. Thoughts of love are constructive of brotherhood, peace, friendship, and happiness."

A happy and cheerful person can create something; a miserable person would always aim at destroying something. Aanandam aims to make the student happy and creative.

National Education policy 2020 envisages a holistic education which involves intellectual, aesthetic, social, physical, emotional and moral development of the student. It aims at encouraging creativity and innovation, critical thinking and higher order thinking among students. It emphasises problem solving attitude, team work, communication skills, in-depth learning and mastery of curricula across fields, social and moral awareness, etc. besides general engagement and enjoyment of learning.

A holistic and multi-disciplinary education would aim to develop all capacities of the students to bring out all-around human beings that possess critica21st-centuryry capacities across arts, sciences, social sciences, technical and vocational fields. The students should have real-lifefe exposure through interaction with the communities around them.

At each stage of learning, skills and values should be imbibed through engaging processes. Aanandam gives the opportunity for experiential learning while utilizing the knowledge gained in different subjects throughout the academic career.

In Aanandam the classroom transactions will shift towards social sensitivity-oriented learning. The assessment/evaluation tools as desired in the new education policy will shift from conventional written examination to the assessment of social sensitivity, empathy, and dispositions. The whole emphasis will be on bringing out community leadership qualities as an outcome, ultimately aiming at the generation of happiness in the society, surroundings, and the learner.

Aanandam will give the opportunity to the learner for greater in-depth study real-life problems, critical thinking and greater attention problem-solving instead of complaining.

It is a concept of joyful learning. While interacting with the community groups, the students get to know the socio-cultural and economic realities of the community. They get the opportunity to be aware of the hardships of deprived sections of theiety in villages and slums. The students while doing the project work of Aanandam interact with people of all the generations, creeds, classes and genders. They get to have a broader and in depth understanding of gender specific problems. They can know more about the status of women, conditions of the old people, specially abled persons, children, girl child in different pockets of the society.

Aanandam adopts a cross curricular approach that utilises various aspects of arts and culture also in executions of the group project work. During Aanandam Diwas the students will demonstrate their project work invarious forms - Nukkad Natak, songs, poetry declamations etc. This will give an opportunity to the students for public performance. Thus Aanandamwill also upgrade their speaking skills with the added advantage of joyful learning with full involvement.

Aanandam would evolve the goodness hidden in the students, turning them into socially responsible, happy human beings. Aanandam would lay a strong foundation of a happy society.

The world today is countenancing volatility and uncertainty in the system on almost all fronts, whether it is social, economic, political or medical. During the global pandemic almost all families in the world faced the worst of the times. This has changed the world view of most of the people living in the world. Almost everyone underwent despair and depression during the covid pandemic when the whole medical world was in fix about the cure of the disease. Growing inclination towards war to settle scores like Russia - Ukraine war, has made things worse in terms of peace and stability. Similarly, the world is facing the ever growing problem of climate change, increasing pollution and depleting natural resources. The students need to know the gravity of the problem and try to find solutions to the problem. The students would use their imaginative and creative faculties to give certain solutions for water conservation, energy saving etc.

The crisis situation created by pandemics demands a collaborative approach towards the pandemic management. The pandemic has not only affected the people physically but also mentally. People who lost their loved ones, who lost their jobs and business during this crisis period are facing lots of mental problems.

They need support, love and care. The students can collaboratively give some solutions at such critical periods. Aanandam gives such opportunities to the students to evolve their human side which is hidden within and which never comes out due to our stress on theoretical knowledge and exams and evaluation based on that. World now needs more aggressively good human beings. Therefore, Aanandam is certainly going to help the society by grooming human qualities among the students. Students need to be aware and inquisitive towards day to day problems of the community, of the family and they need to develop a problem-solving attitude.

Their empathetic quotient has to be enhanced. Aanandam assesses students not on the basis of theoretical knowledge but on the basis of their compassionate empathetic socially responsible attitudes.

The human qualities are nurtured through the contents of this course: Aanandam Diary, Aanandam Day and Community service-related group projects. People equate happiness with short term immediate gratification of needs but that happiness is not long-lasting. It is short-term and sensory happiness also termed Hedonia. Self-fulfilling happiness is long lasting. It lies in giving, caring and kindness. These attributes are valued in the material world also. As only one who is compassionate, collaborative, empathetic problem solver is an asset for any organisation also.

Aanandam course will let the students connect with the inner world of consciousness, will let them discover their own potential which gives real self- fulfilment and happiness. Aanandam thus tackles the problem of increased mental illnesses due to a stressful lifestyle.

To achieve the aspirational goals of the 21st Century including SDG 4 it is necessary that the youth of our country should be groomed through education into socially responsible citizens as well as one who understands the problems of the country, who tries to give indigenous solutions to the problems using modern technology and know-how. Aanandam will not only tap the creative potential but will also help in the development of cognitive capacities i.e. critical thinking problem-solving. It will harness the hidden emotional and empathetic quotient of the students in community interactions.

In our Ancient wisdom - Vidya has been defined as that which liberates – "Ya Vidya Sa Vimuktaye". Here Vimukti has a deep meaning, though in simple words it is self-realisation.

Aanandam is in consonance with this definition of 'Vidya' or education. Achieving happiness is the ultimate aim of life. Whatever we do is for getting happiness only, but with the passage of time and the progress of civilization, most of us have put happiness on the lower rung of the ladder of aspirations. Our youth is caught in a mad race of getting higher and higher packages of salary and instead of getting happiness they end up getting stressed out and frustrated. They are cut off from their surroundings. They don't have any idea about the problems of the community. They are enticed towards the glamour of the virtual world.

Lot of examples of Ancient Indian wisdom, our rich cultural traditions remain simply unobserved. While interacting in the village or mohalla the students will spend some time there. They will come across such examples; they will learn about them while doing the study for their projects.

Aanandam is an amalgamation of the courses the student is learning in his degree course and whatever is learned in school and from the surroundings.

Aanandam recognises the uniqueness of every individual student. Through this course the student will be able to identify his capabilities and will harness that in doing the project work in real-life situations.

Aanandam compliments the academic content of any course by providing a non-academic platform to express the creativity and utilising the knowledge earned in different subjects.

Aanandam provides a platform for the assimilation of the knowledge acquired in different subjects, by bringing it down to utilising it in the field. While doing the project a multi-disciplinary approach will be used for solving the problems in real-life situations - For example - A community problem has sociological, ecological, economic, cultural, political, historical, and anthropological aspects. The students in a group wouldtry to understand the problem holistically and then would suggest a solution.

Thus Aanandam is not limited to one subject but it involves multidisciplinary interaction.

Aanandam would help the students in conceptual understanding of real life situations. The problems around us need critical thinking that will leads to creative solutions.

Aanandam focuses on real happiness generated through giving, sharing and caring. Over the years we have learnt that ethics cannot be taught from the books. Ethics cannot be instilled by solely emphasising on its academic aspect. Ethics can be long lasting only when it evolves from within. When the students interact with the community, try to understand their struggles, their lifestyles, their deprivations, the divisions on the basis of class, caste, gender, and religion, then they realise the realities of life and this serious interaction helps in making them more human. Empathy, pluralism, equality, justice, social responsibility, respect for public property, scientific temper, respecting the dignity of everyone etc. are the natural outcomes of this course.

The project work would also give the students an opportunity to learn the local language, empowering them linguistically.

It will result in better communication skills, teamwork, proactive leadership qualities, cooperation, and resilience.

Aanandam gives flexibility in choosing the subject of project work and autonomy to the group to decide how to do a project.

Aanandam ensures universal participation of the students.

Chapter 2

Ancient Indian Education System and Aanandam

In Ancient India the purpose of education was liberation. Our ancient education system aimed at holistic development of the student which took care of the inner and the outer world. The holistic education included physical, intellectual and spiritual aspects of life of an individual. It consisted of three main components:

1. **Shravan (Listening)** i.e. acquiring the knowledge through listening
2. **Manan (Reflection)-** Learning through deep thinking, analysing and inferring
3. **Nididhyasana-** Application of assimilating and applying the learning in the real life

In Gurukuls the education was imparted in the vicinity of Nature. The students thus got holistic education that had equal emphasis on the external as well as internal world. This type of education led to character building mastering the art of self-control. It made the students socially empathetic also. Students in the ancient education system could understand the importance of nature and environment. In the Gurukul there was a great respect for the gurus (teachers). The Guru and Shishyas lived together and they had a very strong relationship. The guru imparted education in various subjects which are necessary for life as well as for spiritual progress of the student. The ancient education system gave due importance to complexities of life and thought about how to survive in adverse circumstances. The whole ancient Indian wisdom related to political, social, technical or cultural has in fact evolved after experimentations done for survival. Since the emergence of human civilization different sets of people have contributed differently in science, technology, art, craft, architecture, agriculture etc. After deep interactions with the people, nature and environment. Medical treatises of Charak, Sushruta, Arth Shastra of Kautilya, Ashtadhyayi of Panini, Yog Sutra of Patanjali and many more treasures of knowledge were outcomes of holistic education system. Our ancient Indian knowledge is a treasure trove of science, medicine, technology, architecture, various arts & crafts, dance & music. This knowledge was not achieved in man-made laboratories but it was achieved through deep meditation and using all the inner faculties by the seers.

By introducing Aanandam in the curriculum of education today we try to revive and re-introduce our original traditions of learning. Inspired by the ancient education system of learning, Aanandam provides interaction-based learning for the students. It provides the platform for application of the knowledge gained in different subjects in the classroom, through peers and surroundings in solving real life problems. While doing the project work there are chances that some innovations, inventions or discoveries happen which will in turn solve the problems of the community.

> *"The school should help its young people to discover their vocations and responsibilities, and not merely cram their minds with facts and technical knowledge; it should be the soil in which they can grow without fear, happily and integrally."*
>
> \- J. Krishnamurti

Chapter 3
Volunteering and Benevolence

Benevolence is the characteristic element of humanity

- Confucius

Dalai Lama says "The intelligent way to be selfish is to work for the welfare of others."

Small acts of benevolence when done by many are sure to solve the multiple problems of the world. We see all around so many people who are less fortunate to live a comfortable life. There are people who are still struggling for basic needs of life namely food, shelter, clothing and health. World economic surveys point out at glaring income disparities. Such socio - economic inequalities have a potential to disturb the equilibrium and peace of the society. Therefore, to enjoy a peaceful life it"s necessary that the people around us should also be in a comfortable position. This explains the pragmatic need of volunteerism by those who have skill, ability, time or resources.

Kofi Annan (former UN Secretary General) says "If our hopes of building a better and safer world are to become more than wishful thinking, we will need an engagement of volunteers more than ever."

Our youth has the capacity as well as intention to use their creative abilities in the larger interest. Natalie Portman (an eminent Hollywood actor) says "Our generation has the ability and the responsibility to make our ever more connected world a more hopeful, stable and peaceful place."

Aanandam course majorly emphasises on proactively volunteering for making our society healthier and happier. It has four basic features:

1. Karuna (Kindness)
2. Maitri (Friendliness, Benevolence)
3. Sahridayam (Heartful)
4. Srijanam (Creativity)

Karuna and Maitri are the most important virtues of a human being. Upanishads as well as Patanjali Yoga Sutras highlight these virtues. Karuna and Maitri are interdependent. It signifies benevolence, kindness towards everyone and compassion towards the sufferings of others as one's own. Karuna and Maitri promote Srijanam (Creativity) and Srijanam leads to ultimate Aanandam (Peace). A person gets empathetic joy in the happiness of others. When the student interacts with the community when they try to understand their way of life and their day to day problems then their empathetic quotient is going to increase, in other words attributes of Karuna and Maitri will evolve. This unconditional, unselfish friendliness will generate mental equanimity and acceptance. This will reduce the negativity and the habit of cribbing for any unfavourable circumstance. Chanakya says he who nurtures benevolence for all creatures within his heart overcomes all difficulties and will be the recipient of all types of riches at every step. Every act of benevolence or Maitri and Karuna generates deep satisfaction and joy. Mahatma Gandhi says the simplest acts of kindness are by far more powerful than a thousand heads bowing in prayer.

Everyone in this world wants to enjoy life. All the philosophies have evolved in search of happiness. But we also know that happiness cannot flourish in isolation. The whole universe reflects interdependence. Every living being is an inseparable part of the ecosystem interdependently connected to each other. Therefore, it's necessary that students should understand their role and duties towards society, humanity and the environment as a whole.

Volunteerism among youth have a number of benefits:

It gives the opportunity to the young minds to use their skills and attributes for helping others. It promotes positive belongingness in the community. The students who volunteer proactively become more empathetic. Such young persons are more productive members of society, they are in really happier and more contented. Thus volunteerism simultaneously is beneficial for the society and the person who volunteers for helping others. There are studies which show that youth volunteerism contributes to identity development, enhanced self - esteem, evolution of an empathetic personality and overall development of the attributes that contribute to enhancement in employability. Voluntary activities expand the plain of interactions as while doing such activities they meet a variety of individuals from different backgrounds.

Volunteerism is the core of Aanandam. We firmly believe that the young minds are full of untapped energy. This energy needs to be channelized. The youth should be given the opportunities where they can express their hidden feelings of kindness, love and sharing and use their untapped energies. Aanandam provides them this opportunity of volunteerism. In our education system we have a tight schedule of classes of different subjects followed by exams. So there is no time for volunteering and therefore our students are deprived of the chance of volunteering. Aanandam has been included in the curriculum of technical education to provide a structured scope for volunteerism. The faculty acting as mentors of Aanandam are the facilitators and guide for helping and choosing a voluntary activity, for solving the practical difficulties and logistics and making the whole voluntary activity a joyful experience. There is also provision of rewarding good volunteering activities in Aanandam.

The volunteer experience of the student is going to add great value to the CV. The employers of good companies prefer people who have volunteering experience. Even for higher studies also volunteering helps and it's an important factor in securing admission and a scholarship. The scholarships are generally awarded to students who show community leadership skills. Volunteerism generates generosity among the youth. There is no dearth of examples of volunteerism around. It is an act of sharing and giving whether it is time, once abilities or skills or wealth. In the words of Opportunity Nation, "There is mounting evidence that volunteering, participating in service projects, and other forms of community involvement are more than feel good activities. They can contribute to better outcomes for youth and for communities." Volunteerism brings inner transformation amongst youth. In this fast changing world where every year the speed of internet is changing, we need to protect our society from maladies of the speed. This is not possible without involving our youth who are filled with fresh ideas. Therefore, there should be a platform where the young students interact with the problems of the community and apply their minds to solve it.

> *Every man must decide whether he will walk in the light of creative altruism or in the darkness of destructive selfishness*
>
> \- Martin Luther King Jr.

Chapter 4

Volunteering Immersion for Students at

MAHE Manipal- An Institute of Eminence

There's a social responsibility every institution must fulfil, not merely to better public image but to genuinely do something for the less fortunate. No institution can turn a blind eye when it comes to social responsibility particularly when those in need are in close proximity. Manipal Academy of Higher Education (MAHE), a global education hub and an Institute of Eminence, was always committed to serving the interest of the needy communities around the University. In 2007, it was decided to take University's commitment to social cause in a more organized manner and therefore, the endeavour to reach out to more and more people became simpler and effective.

That was how Volunteer Services Organization (VSO), the social unit of MAHE came into existence on September 14, 2007. The purpose of starting VSO and what it meant for all those who would join it was amply clear – serving voluntarily. With that in mind, VSO took shape rather quickly. Students, faculty, staff and their spouses all joined the organization to serve a cause selflessly. It became a platform to help the needy in various ways. In the process, it also provided the volunteers an opportunity to gain new skills, work as a team and, most importantly, to become a better person.

With a strength of over 7000 registered volunteers from various constituent colleges at Manipal & Mangalore, VSO undertakes projects which cover community, social, organizational and soft skills avenues.

Clean Manipal Campaign, visit to slums of Udupi and Mangalore, blood donation camps, visit to paediatric wards of Kasturba Hospitals, Kannada classes (spoken), birthday celebrations at orphanages, organizing fund raising shows and organizing Daan Utsav-joy of giving week are some of the programs which have had a tremendous impact on the communities in and around Manipal and Mangalore.

Mission Statement

VSO aims to develop the spirit of selfless service by responding to the community"s needs, addressing the issues of society, and developing the leadership and learning skills of the volunteers. Students, faculty, and staff strive to ameliorate the conditions of the impoverished and the less fortunate. We come together in hopes of forging a path to a better society.

Objectives of the Practice

Volunteer Services Organization is the social upliftment umbrella of MAHE which aims to provide a platform for students, faculty and faculty spouses to volunteer in and around Manipal. It aspires to inculcate the spirit of selflessness, nurture the ability to give, and mold future leaders. The organization provides volunteers for various University events throughout the year, and is instrumental in carrying out multiple, weekly community outreach visits to slums, old age homes, orphanages, schools and hospital wards. Additionally, beach cleaning, cleanliness drives around Manipal, health awareness camps and blood donation drives are also carried out. Through these visits, VSO has continued to create a difference in the lives of people in the Udupi-Manipal community through sustained interactions as well as instill empathy, kindness, sensitivity and courage among its volunteers.

The Context

Volunteer Services Organization employs a unique and easily replicable model to any college or University intending to involve its students in various acts of giving. It firmly believes that the essence of education is to be of service to the community. As per the National Education Policy, 2020, VSO aims to integrate the concept of United Nation"s Sustainable Development Goals (SDG) in each of its activities. Every visit is curated keeping in mind at least one of the 17 SDG"s, with the most prominent being quality education, and clean water and sanitation. Being University students, most of the volunteers are involved in technical or health-care research and VSO hopes to harmonize volunteering and innovation to provide a unique platform to apply research and formulate practical solutions towards serving the community at large. It exposes volunteers to the extraordinary domain of social entrepreneurship, with the aim of bringing the youth together in an endeavour to develop a more caring and a successful nation.

The Practice

The Volunteer Services Organization (VSO) started on September 17, 2007 with an aim to provide opportunity to students and staff to volunteer and to instill a sense of responsibility in them towards the society. The core objectives of VSO are to respond to the community needs; to address the issues of the society; to develop leadership potential of students and to enhance student learning through collaboration. The goal of learning through community service in VSO is to combine service and learning objectives with an intention of changing both the recipient and the provider of the service. Service tasks and organized opportunities that relate the service task to self-reflection, self-discovery, and the acquisition and comprehension of values, skills, and knowledge material result in changes in the provider. Every college keeps a slot for VSO presentation during the orientation of the course. During the presentation, the details about the organization, its structure, process of joining and benefit at personal and professional level is shared. Following that, students register at the website and after an approval from the chief coordinator, they get their user Id and password. Using this user Id and password, they can login to their profile and register for any project which takes places during the weekend. These volunteers, after a specific number of volunteering hours and based on project need, can apply to become a project coordinator. These volunteers are selected to become project coordinator, based on their motivation letter and a personal interview. The project coordinators upload the projects (which are aligned with a specific sustainable development goals (SDGs)) on the website with the details of the project and manage the activities on the day of the project along with the registered volunteers. These project coordinators can later apply to become the student head of the organization as VSO student ambassador. All the activities in VSO is coordinated by the students and mentored by the faculty coordinators from the constituent institutions. The uniqueness of this social wing of the university is 7000+ active volunteers. Every week, 200+ volunteers participate in more than 10 various community projects and contribute 400+ hrs. of volunteering every week. All these volunteering hours are recorded on the VSO website and each volunteer can see the number of hours contributed by them in their profile. Once the volunteers are about to complete their professional course, they can apply for the certificate stating the number of hours. contributed to volunteering. VSO has a sustainable volunteering engagement and has evolved a system over the years for academic volunteering in higher educations in India.

Through this unique opportunity of structured academic volunteering, student gain opportunities to meaningfully engage in community service that benefits the community and also instill a sense of civic and social responsibility within them. This best practice of the university is in line with the National Education Policy 2020 (NEP 2020) which lays strong emphasis on community engagement and community service for community building.

Regular Programmes

Weekly Programmes

Jyothi - Visit to ASARE, school for special children (Sunday, 4 pm-6 pm)

Sanjeevani – Visit to Paediatric Ward of Kasturba Hospital (Sunday, 4 pm- 6 pm)

Aarambh - Sri Krishna Balaniketan, An Orphanage (Sunday, 4 pm- 6pm)

Clean Manipal Campaign (Sunday, 5pm-7pm)

Blood Donation Camp (Sunday, 9 pm-5 pm)

Parivartana- Visit to Udupi Slums (Sunday, 9 am – 11 am)

Beach Clean Up Drive (Sunday, 6.30 am – 9.30 am)

Khushi- Visit to Nittur Balamandir for girls (Saturday, 3 pm – 5 pm)

Village Adoption Programme (Sunday, 9 am – 11 am)

Visit to Academy General School (Saturday, 3 pm – 5 pm)

Vidya – A visit to Namma Bhoomi, home for underprivileged (Sunday, 9 am – 11 am)

Yodha – Visit to Paediatric Cancer Ward of the hospital (Sunday, 4 pm-6 pm)

Akansha – visit to home for cancer affected children (Sunday, 4 pm-6 pm)

Special Programmes

Spoken Kannada Classes

Birthday Celebration at Orphanages (every month, last Sunday)

Health Camps for underprivileged people

Collection drives (clothes, stationary, toys)

SPARSH – fund raising cultural show

TARANG – a kite flying festival

DaanUtsav – a joy of giving week

Appreciation

Volunteering at VSO is a selfless service but appreciation through a certificate for the service plays a big motivation for volunteers to go an extra mile. At VSO, all projects are time defined, and the time spend by a volunteer are documented through an in-house online system designed & developed by volunteers. Once a volunteer participates in a project, a certain number of hours (as defined for that particular project) gets added to his VSO account. Once he completes 32 hours of volunteering, the volunteer can apply for a VSO certificate in the online system. The certificate also gives an option to mention any two projects of their choice. Further VSO certificate are categorized under the following categories:

>=32 hours to < 63 hours: Bronze Certificate

>=64 hours to < 95 hours: Silver Certificate

>=96 hours: Gold Certificate

Volunteers having >=96 hours of service are also eligible to receive a letter of recommendation (if required) from the head of VSO.

Volunteer can apply for a VSO certificate once during their entire academic year of study. However, volunteer can download their contributions (date, projects, time spent) at any time if they require the credentials from the online portal.

Evidence of Success

The evidence of success can be seen in growing number of active volunteers in VSO which meaningfully engage themselves in community activities in spite of their busy academic schedule. Over the years, the VSO alumni received international study scholarships, have joined and worked in social and development sectors and have ventured into social entrepreneurship. They all attribute this to the exposure they receive in VSO where silos were broken, and they learned collaboratively with, from and about each other. This engagement gave them an opportunity to see the world with the different lens and contribute back to the society. VSO, MAHE is seen as frontrunner in academic volunteering by the leaders of social and development sectors where it sets an example of constant volunteer engagement in delivering the collaborative projects. The volunteering journey which volunteers undertake in VSO, gives them an opportunity to connect, an opportunity to develop, an opportunity to grow, an opportunity to self-discover, an opportunity to build a career in social work, an opportunity to make someone happy and an opportunity to create a better tomorrow time.

Problems Encountered and Resources Required

As a division of MAHE, VSO operates on the Manipal and Mangalore campuses and recently started in Bengaluru. Our activities are restricted to the areas surrounding these locations. VSO has yet to explore partnerships with local NGOs that might strengthen its efforts. Sadly, there are very few NGOs working on social and environmental concerns around these campuses. VSO has collaborated with national-level NGOs on a number of projects, including Daan Utsav and the National Youth Conference. These partnerships should be continued and extended to weekly projects.

The secret to the volunteers' long-term development is consistent mentorship. At the moment, each institution has a college coordinator who serves as a mentor. The time offered by the mentors to carry out different initiatives is being constrained by their various duties and responsibilities as well as their personal and professional priorities. College coordinators should have regular chances for training and development along with monetary benefits.

Impact of VSO activities (Average 3 years)

Sl. No.	Target Group	Project Name & Details (Impact)	Outcome of the impact (Number of people benefitted)
1	Sick Children admitted in hospital	Sanjeevani – Weekly volunteering activity at Paediatric Ward of Kasturba Hospital	100 visits (2hr each) were arranged over 3 years involving 2,000 volunteers and targeting nearly 10,000 people. Sick children actively participated in all feel-good activity. Parents & children look forward to volunteer visit every week
2	Special people (Mentally retarded people)	Jyothi – weekly volunteering activity at Asare home for special children	Nearly 1800 volunteers participated in 90 visits (2 hr each) to home for special home and conducted vocational training for well-being of the people and to remove their social stigma. Inmates became more confident and mingle with students and started working at various places
3	Orphan children	Arambh & Sandhya – weekly volunteering activity at orphanages	100 visits were conducted by 2500 volunteers to orphanages to conduct computer education, soft skills training, English teaching. Children become more confident, fluent in English and handling computers

4	Socio economically deprived people	Muskaan - Weekly activity at Slums by volunteers	64 visits to nearly slums involving 1280 volunteers were conducted for training the slum kids, imparting education. School enrolment increased and healthy practices were observed among slum dwellers
5	Old people residing in Old age home	Asha – weekly activity at old age home by volunteers	300 volunteers visited old age home nearly 30 times and interacted & spend time with inmates. They actively participate in activities and look forward to the visit
6	Students, Faculty	Spoken Kannada Classes conducted by volunteers	8 courses were conducted involving 1200 people to impart spoken kannada education and promote the culture of the state
7	General Public	Clean Manipal Campaign – weekly Swaccha Bharat Abhiyan by volunteers	60 visits involving 1200 volunteers cleaned the surrounding areas, spread awareness & installed dustbins.
8	Students, Faculty	Come and Donate blood - Blood Donation Camp every week by volunteers	Nearly 900 volunteers donated blood
9	Haemophilic patients, Premature babies, special people	Tarang – annual fund raising kite flying fund activity by volunteers	Nearly 2 Lakh rupees were raised and donated for the patients benefit. Awareness was spread during the events
10	General Public	DaanUtsav – joy of giving week between Oct 2-8	Nearly 70 projects involving nearly 20,000 givers were planned and implemented over 1 week duration (Oct2-8) over 3 years

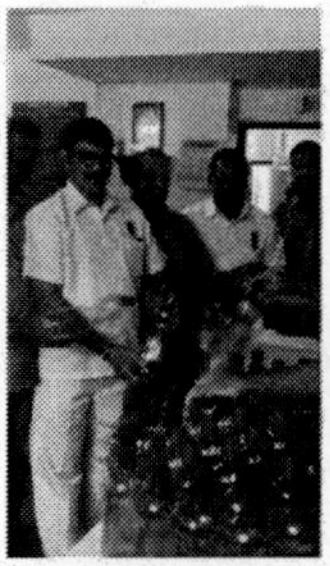

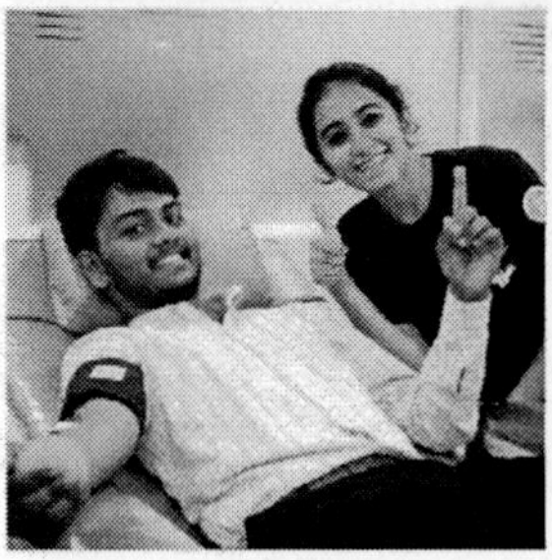

Compiled by
Dr. Anup Naha
Chief Coordinator, VSO
Associate Professor
MAHE, Manipal
anup.naha@manipal.edu

Chapter 5

Aanandam and Environmental Sustainability

"The Greatest Threat to Our Planet is the Belief That Someone Else Will Save It"

- Robert Swan

Today the world is grappling with the outcomes of modern notions of growth and development. Since the industrial revolution we have been made to think that more and more industrialization would lead to economic development and the happiness of society. But while evaluating the development we didn't take into account the cost in terms of depletion of natural resources and harmful gas emissions that pollute the environment which is disastrous for all living beings. Climate change is a big environmental challenge. It has affected the lives of millions of people, flora and fauna. The frequency of droughts, forest fires, floods, earthquakes is increasing continuously. Steps are needed to sustain with such environment. Pollution problems are ever increasing and are adversely impacting the health of everyone. Interventions are needed to reduce the causes of the pollution like minimising the use of plastics, chemicals etc. There is need to conserve energy. According to the UNO calculation, 13% of the world population lacks access to electricity and three billion people are dependent on fossil fuels for their day to day needs. Therefore, energy efficient equipments are needed and also the ways to use the renewable energy sources have to be searched. The availability of food and drinking water is also getting scarce. Sustainable solutions are needed to solve this problem. So there is no dearth of problems which demand immediate solutions. The Nobel Peace prize winner the first African women Wangari Maathai rightly says, "The environment and the economy are really both two sides of the same coin. If we cannot sustain the environment, we cannot sustain ourselves."

Traditionally Indian society had always valued scarce resources like water, soil or energy. We had been in the habit of reusing, recycling and reducing to preserve our resources. Philosophically we always emphasised on the notion of „Aparigrah" i.e. not collecting more than what we need for living a life. There are examples of prudent ways of conservation of water, conservation of soil through rotation of crops and the like. We need to be aware of our strong traditions of understanding the environment and preserve it.

With this background in mind Aanandam course has been formulated in an all-inclusive manner so that in Aanandam Diary as well as in Group Projects the students become conversant with the environmental problems and can imagine and think creatively about resolving them.

Individual and community efforts can result in large scale positive impact on the environment. One can take up a patch of wasteland lying in the college campus or anywhere in the locality. By small and consistent efforts that patch can be turned into a beautiful green area full of trees with birds and butterflies perching on them. Some other can take up a task of developing some alternatives to the plastics which are used in day to day lives. If the young minds are perturbed by scarcity of water, energy or some other environmental problem and are determined to solve them, then there might be many innovative solutions. We come across so many good environmental stories in newspapers and media. Recently there was a story of a person from Samastipur Bihar. A 33-year-old Shri Rajesh Kumar Suman started a unique coaching centre which charged from its students 18 plant saplings as fees. What a way to give back, educating the children and protecting the environment at the same time! In another story a visually challenged person every monsoon does rain water harvesting for 1 lakh litres of rain water. Similarly, in Mumbai an artist Haribabu Naatesan used 25 tons E-waste for his art work. Such stories are the examples of creativity that contributes to environmental sustainability.

Aanandam gives ample opportunity to the students to be sensitive and observant about the environmental issues. The students can take up any of the environmental problems as a topic of their project work and can use their mental capabilities to give certain solutions for environmental sustainability.

> *"The unselfish effort to bring cheer to other will be the*
> *beginning of a happier life for our ourselves"*
>
> - Hellen Keller

Chapter 6

AANANDAM DIARY

Today abundant knowledge is easily available simply by pressing some keys on a smartphone or a computer. Very less scope is left for expressing ourselves through our original thoughts. So something is left frustrated within. Writing by hand in a diary helps in boosting the creative urge. Aanandam diary is a very important part of this course. It requires that one should observe his / her deeds daily. In fact, everyone does some good deed every day, but it is overlooked. The students will keep a watch on their deeds and pick up one good deed done to be recorded by hand in the Aanandam Diary. This task will be done on a daily basis. The Diary will be discussed in the Aanandam period. The Aanandam period should be there in the time table every day. It can be a short period of 25 minutes and will be kept as an extension of any of the subject periods. This way Aanandam course will not require any special faculty or any particular dedicated period.

There are a number of benefits of observing a good deed and recording it by hand in Aanandam Diary. Writing by hand helps in increasing mindfulness similar to meditation. When the student observes his / her deeds and records one good deed in the Diary, it gives a sense of self fulfilment and joy of giving. When it becomes a habit of doing a good deed and writing it by hand it will tap the hidden goodness concealed within. This helps in evolution of Karuna and Maitri i.e. Kindness and Friendliness, turning a person into a compassionate human being. At present the whole system focuses on punishing the wrongdoings, making laws and prisons for punishments but nothing has been done to tap the goodness which is already there and evolve a person into a good human being. Aanandam Diary provides this opportunity to our students.

There were also suggestions that the student can record their good deeds on a smartphone or a laptop using the keyboard but then the purpose of this part of Aanandam would have been defeated as it would have reduced the sense of ownership and belongingness. When the person writes by hand then a particular part of the brain is used and thus the thought of good deeds gets endorsed and imprinted there. Another great benefit of Aanandam Diary is that when one sits to read it at leisure he / she will be impressed by his / her evolution into a good human being.

Recording an Individual Act of Goodness – Each student individually does an „act of goodness" per day and that is recorded in the „**Aanandam diary**". That Diary is shared with the mentor and other students in the assigned time slot.

Glimpses of 'Aanandam diary' maintained by a student

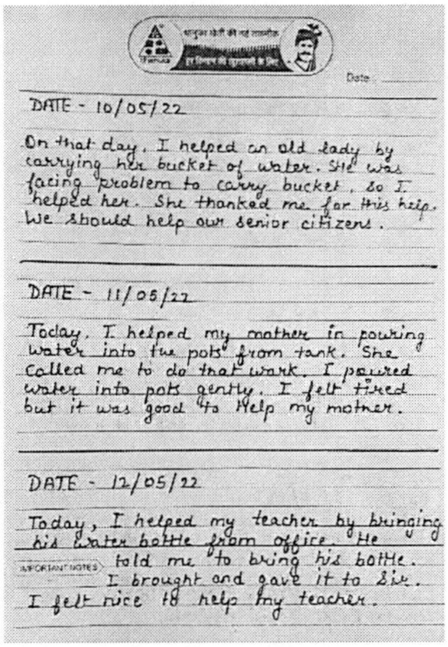

Aanandam Diary will be discussed in the period of Aanandam. The teacher in the class will simply listen to what the students have written in the Diary but will not evaluate and judge any of the incidents written by the students. The role of the teacher is to facilitate and not preach about anything. The purpose behind this is that the student's original ideas should be fostered instead of being suppressed. Students are free to write what they feel is good and in the interest of the society. This will help in bringing out the good human qualities hidden inside a student.

The Aanandam diary is mandatory. The mentor in the class will only record whether the student has recorded an incident of good deed done. There won"t be any marks for Aanandam Diary.

Chapter 7

Aanandam and Community Service

"Without Community Service, we would not have a strong quality of life. It's important to the person who serves as well as the recipient. It's the way in which we ourselves grow and develop."

- Dorothy Height

Today we live in a world where we have access to the remotest corners through the most advanced technology of communication. A huge virtual world has been created by the modern means of communications. Everyone is seen engrossed in their smartphones. But at the same time there is a great neglect of human interaction physically. This abundance of virtual communications has also led to a hollowness in real lives. Our youth, mainly residing in cities, is today deprived of personal touch with the community around them. Most of them have scanty knowledge about the problems of the communities living in slums and small villages. There is a necessity of bringing our students face to-face with the stark realities of community life. There should be exposure to the problems and hardships faced by the deprived sections of society. This is possible only when the students are sensitised towards them by involving them into personal interaction with such groups. Interaction with the community and an exposure to the harsh realities will make the student more imaginative and creative because this will give them the opportunity to think about solving their problems. Interaction with the community and efforts to solve their problems will also increase the empathetic quotient of the student. In fact, their interaction with the community is a win-win situation for both. It will be mutually beneficial. Any invention or discovery originates from the problems of people.

There is an African proverb "If you want to go fast, go alone; but if you want to go far go together"

No education can be complete without involving the community around us. Education has to be linked with life to make it a meaningful education.

How to Interact with the Community for a Community Service Project

For doing a Community Service Project the students should try to build a comfortable level of communication with the members of the community. The first step is to break the ice and build rapport with the persons who are influential in the community.

They should try to understand a general socio- economic background of the community, their day-to-day life through conversations. They should try to create a sense of connection by sharing about themselves and why they are doing a certain project with them. The students should build an understanding about their lifestyle, culture and habits. They should listen to their problems carefully and also should discuss with them about various solutions of the problems. They should be good listener: Listening carefully and without interrupting instantly builds rapport. They should be empathetic to their problems. It"s necessary that the conversations with the community should be in an appropriate language. They should also try to pick some prominent dialectical words to build a good rapport with the community.

Using appropriate and layman's language could be one of the best ways to kick-start a conversation and may help in building rapport faster. Try to inject an element of humour during the conversations to make it lighter.

Body language: Body language is an important element in any communication that uses physical gestures. While talking to various stakeholders and target groups, one should maintain their body posture, eye contact, facial expression in a manner that does not make the other person feel uncomfortable. One should be wary of their body language that signals disinterest, judgement, bias, or any other behaviour that may become a discomfort for the stakeholder or target group into further sharing their thoughts.

Reserve judgement: Withhold your criticism towards any of their thoughts towards various issues and concerns. Share advice only when they request you for that. Emphasise positivity and facilitate openness to their opinion.

Organise group meetings/discussion forum: organise meetings with various stakeholders and provide them opportunities to ask questions, provide testimonies and raise concerns.

Define their role in the collaboration: defining their role and appreciating their presence will develop a feeling of ownership towards the collaboration.

Be visible in local communities: be part of their local events, meetings and forums and engage in their conversation. Be a part of them. Being visible in the community fosters a sense of transparency and trust.

While interacting with the community and discussing their problems with them, the community members learn how to prioritize their problems and find their solutions. They learn to work together for the common good. They would know how to mobilise resources which are already available in the community. In short the community service project done by the students will side by side empower the community also. This will ensure the sustainability of the outcomes of development programs of government and non-government agencies. The entire community service project will thus be an educational process for the students as well as the community. The students would come to know about the scarcity of resources and would learn to value them. They would learn the importance of conservation through community participation. No wonder community service project might result in great discoveries, innovative ideas for future startups and enterprises.

Chapter 8

Aanandam Day

How to make learning a Celebration

"I slept and dreamt the life was a joy. I awoke and saw that life was service. I acted and behold, service was a joy"

- Rabindra Nath Tagore

Aanandam in reality makes learning a celebration. The students work in teams in tandem with Nature. They use their creative potential. They imagine the ways to solve the problems. They learn a lot while interacting with the community.

Celebrating Aanandam Day

Aanandam day will be celebrated once in a month in the college campus. All the students and the faculty will participate. If the institution wishes, it can invite some persons of repute and NGOs also to show the activities of the students done under Aanandam. The students will display their work done in their respective group projects in the form of charts, nukkad natak, declamations, paintings etc. They would use their talents to exhibit their work. Aanandam day will be full of fun and celebrations. The projects displayed on Aanandam day would be given marks by an evaluation committee made by the head of the institution. Aanandam day will be celebrated every month and thus there will be continuous evaluation of the group project. Aanandam day also gives the opportunity to the students and mentors to discuss the problems, if any faced while doing the project work.

Chapter 9

How to do a Group Project-Work

Aanandam is a holistic course that will help in the evolution of the student into a human being with a balanced outlook towards the external and internal world. It helps in Growth of the individual in harmony with the community and the environment.

It is a course that uses the faculties of a student for the healthy growth of a society. It gives opportunity for experiential learning, explorations of community life, its problems and using the learned skills in solving the problems. It provides a vast scope for critical thinking and innovative solutions. If the students want help or guidance regarding some problems in execution of the project work, then the mentors should give a wholehearted support.

The findings of some of the Aanandam projects may also result in some great sociological and economic surveys of a particular pocket of the community or social group.

The solutions suggested by the students in their project works can be precursors of some important inventions, innovations, startups and some policy decisions.

The Project work will have five phases:

(i) Introductory phase - preliminary interaction with community.

(ii) Inquisitive phase - inquisitive about the problem.

(iii) Discussion & Analysis phase – Discussing & Analysing the problems with the community and among the group members.

(iv) Discovery phase - discovering the indigenous solutions.

(v) Solution phase - innovation, idea generation, critical thinking with focus on concepts, ideas applications and problem solving.

Every individual member will have a piece of the task. The Members will work collaboratively towards the object of the project. Every student member will get a sufficient chance to show their leadership skills. Project work will be an example of collaborative leadership.

Interacting with the community

The students will do a brief study of the community group they take up for the project. They will try to understand the cultural aspects. They will pick up the local dialectics, to make their communication effective. They will observe the eating habits and other aspects of routine life. They will try to understand the economic aspect of a family - the sources of livelihood, consumption pattern, daily expenses. Their awareness about Government Welfare Schemes etc. This brief study will form the 1st chapter of the project report.

Selection of the problem

Methodology - (i) interaction with community – the interactions with community leaders, women groups, youth, elders need to be discussed in the report substantiated with photographs.

(a) Picking up the problem.

(b) Defining the problem.

(c) Discussion about the problem.

(d) Analysing the causes.

Solution - Suggesting the solutions:

Procedure, Planning, Execution should be explained in the project report.

Project Examples -

(i) Studying the artisans and craftsmen in an artisan community.

(ii) A village ward - problem of electricity/water/roads etc.

(iii) A slum - Problem of sanitation and hygiene.

(iv) Problem of livelihood - suggesting some solution like formation of self-help groups, skill training, computer literacy etc.

(v) Problem of addiction to tobacco on the college campus.

(vi) Problems related to malnutrition - spreading awareness about anaemia and other deficiencies - eating the right food. The project can be taken up in an Aanganwadi.

(vii) Problems related to physically challenged persons.

(viii) Problem of barren land - it can be the college campus itself.

(ix) Agricultural students can take up the project of teaching organic farming to the natives of a place.

(x) Understanding the problems related to old aged persons. Old age homes can also be taken up as a subject of the project.

Project Report Writing

The project will be written in two parts:

(i) Synopsis

(ii) Main Project Report

(i) **Synopsis: -** The synopsis of the project to be undertaken will be written before actually starting the project work. It will contain

a. Introduction

b. Objectives of the project work

c. Area of the project work

d. Targeted beneficiaries

e. Problem selection

f. Methodology / Procedure Adopted

g. Help from Government / Non-Government Organisations

The synopsis will briefly explain their project work in 15-20 pages. It will be signed by all the students in the group. The mentor teacher will be the guide of the project.

(ii) Main Project Report:-

The main project report will be written under following heads:

1. Preface
2. Acknowledgement
3. Chapters
    - Introduction of the project
    - Objective of the project
    - The procedure adopted
    - Activities and Timeline

- Description of Social Interaction Observation and Experience while doing the project substantiated with photographs and media clippings (if there is any)
- Achievements of the project - Benefits to the community
- Individual Contribution of the Group Members
- Conclusion and Learning outcome of the project

The report will be signed by all the participants, students. The mentor teacher will sign the project report before submission.

It"s necessary to give a brief description of the community where the project work is being undertaken. This introduction about the community will be discussed under the following heads:

A.(i) Socio cultural Background of the community including - status of women.

(ii) Geographical location mentioning river, nala, conditions of the roads, plantation etc. other dominant features.

(iii) Economic condition - sources of livelihood, substantiated with photographs.

There can also be some projects which don't involve community interactions like some technical / engineering projects. In that case a brief description about the usefulness of the project for the community or any other larger entity should be made a part of the project report.

There is no restriction in selection of the topics for the projects. The purpose of the group project is basically to develop the leadership qualities and problem-solving attitude among the students. The teachers will act as facilitators and not as judgemental entities. The group project work in Aanandam aims at evolving the imaginative and creative faculties of the students.

Model Project Reports

Project Report I

1. **Introduction: -** This Group Project has been undertaken in Aanandam. Ten students will work together on this project in the current session with the aim to bring about positive social change by impacting the lives of poor women of Devpura area of Bundi. The student group shortlisted 50 poor women with basic literacy to carry out the Project objectives. The aim was to empower the selected women by imparting a variety of entrepreneurial skills such as accounting, internet access, and personal financial management with the aim that these sessions would enable the women to improve the sustainability of their micro-businesses and help them become more economically independent.

2. **Objectives of the Project: -**

a. Understand the challenges that the poor women of Devpura Kachhi Basti, Bundi face in their daily lives.

b. Teach them a variety of entrepreneurial skills such as accounting, internet access and personal financial management.

c. Enable the women to improve the sustainability of their micro businesses and help them become more economically independent.

3. **Area identified for the work:-** Devpura Kachhi Basti, Bundi

4. **Target beneficiary: -** 50 Poor women of Devpura Kachhi Basti, Bundi.

5. **Methodology/Procedure to be followed: -**

a. The student group will work in collaboration with an NGO I-India.

b. The group of ten students will further divide into 5 pairs. Each pair will adopt 10 women from the 50 shortlisted women. Each student pair will interact with the 10 women of their group for one and a half hour on a daily basis and teach the women a variety of entrepreneurial skills such as accounting, internet access and personal financial management

6. **Name of the Government body/ NGO involved:-** in collaboration with an NGO I-India.

Signature of the Students

1. ....
2. ....
3. ....
4. ....
5. ....
6. ....
7. ....
8. ....
9. ....

Project Report II

1. **Introduction: -** This Group Project has been undertaken in Aanandam. Ten students will work together on this project in the current session with the aim to bring about positive social change through innovations in ways of growing vegetables at the College level. The student will experiment with the Hydroponic technique. It is a new age technique to grow crops at a 30% faster rate and with 80% less water and the most interesting part is, the crops do not require soil to grow.

2. **Objectives of the Project:-**

a. Growing seasonal vegetables in College Botanical Garden

b. Growing hydroponic vegetables which require minimum water, fertilizers and can be grown without soil.

c. Supplying the produce to the Red Cross Society, Bundi runs a charity kitchen for poor patients and starving people.

3. **Area identified for the work: -** Growing vegetables for the poor in the College Botanical Garden.

4. **Target beneficiary: -** Poor people who are fed by Red Cross Society, Bundi.

5. **Methodology/Procedure to be followed: -**

a. The student group will work in collaboration with an NGO I-India.

b. The group of ten students will further divide into 5 pairs. Each pair will develop 2 suitable vegetable beds and one hydroponic space to experiment, innovate and grow vegetables requiring less water and fertilizers.

c. Each student pair will put in at least one hour of labour on a daily basis and tend to their vegetable beds. They will choose seasonal vegetables for better results. As mentioned an innovative step would be to grow some vegetables using the Hydroponic method. For this students on the campus will be asked to bring waste plastic bottles and containers from home.

6. Name of the Government body/ NGO involved:- in collaboration with an NGO I-India.

Signature of the Students

1. ....
2. ....
3. ....
4. ....
5. ....
6. ....
7. ....
8. ....
9. ....

Project Report III

1. **Introduction:-** This Group Project has been undertaken in Aanandam. Ten students will work together on this project in the current session with the aim to bring about positive social change through innovations by providing accounting solutions to local vendors and small storekeepers in the Sabzimandi area of Bundi by training them to use the app "bill buddy."

   The app is helpful to generate bills on the voice input mode for small vendors and make records of purchases of customers. The interesting part of the app is that Purchase Bills can be transferred to customers through an e-mode via SMS, email, etc. on the spot, with which customers can track the records of their purchase bill. Vendors can select payment mode during purchases and can see daily, weekly, monthly and even an all-time record of overall usage pattern of payment mode.

   The Student group has chosen to work on this project so as to train and help the vendors in billing, accounting, book keeping and filing taxes thereby mitigating the need and cost to go to an accountant.

2. **Objectives of the Project:-**

a. Train the selected local vendors and small store keepers to download and learn to use an app "bill buddy."

b. Help them to resolve problems related to accounting, billing, book keeping and filing taxes.

3. **Area identified for the work: -** Local vendors and small storekeepers in the Sabzi mandi area of Bundi.

4. **Target beneficiary: -** 25 Selected local vendors and small-store keepers in the Sabzi mandi area of Bundi.

5. **Methodology/Procedure to be followed: -**

The student group will work in collaboration with volunteers of second and third-year Commerce students and an NGO I-India, of Bundi.

a. The group of ten students will further divide into 5 pairs. Each pair will identify five (05) local vendors and small-store keepers in the Sabzi mandi area of Bundi. The pairs will meet the selected groups for an hour on a daily basis. They will train them to learn to use an app "bill buddy." The student groups will help the vendors in billing, accounting, book keeping and filing taxes thereby mitigating the need and cost to go to an accountant.

6. **Name of the Government body/NGO involved:-** in collaboration with I-India, an NGO.

Signature of the Students

1. ....
2. ....
3. ....
4. ....
5. ....
6. ....
7. ....
8. ....
9. ....

EVALUATION OF THE PROJECT WORK

Aanandam emphasises on tapping the hidden potential and evolution of the students instead of learning a subject by rote selective study for exams and getting marks based on role learning. The Aanandam project is to be assessed by the Project Evaluation Committee. The progress of the project would be continuously assessed on the basis of monthly performance on Aanandam Day which will be held every month. No student has to fail in this subject. No concept of competition or comparisons among the students, as every project done and every contribution made by each student is unique. The mentors are supposed to encourage and incentivise the students for their work.

The evaluation system in Aanandam is not based on competition or comparisons. It is based on the belief that competition destroys love and friendliness. Competition involves race against each other and it results in reduction in joyfulness. In Aanandam nobody fails or passes. Every Aanandam project is unique in itself and is valued for the idea and efforts behind the execution of the project. No project is inferior to other projects. There is no concept of an exam for evaluation in Aanandam. It is based on continuous evaluation. Progress of Aanandam projects will be watched every month on Aanandam Day. In a semester there will be six Aanandam Days. In their project reports the students will be showing their activities substantiated with the news clippings and photographs. Grades will be given in the projects. The evaluation will be done to promote creativity, originality and problem-solving approach reflected in the project work.

THE CBCS (CHOICE BASED CREDIT SYSTEM)

The CBCS system offers three types of course choices to the students which are: core, elective and foundation. Of these, the elective subjects have more generic content and aim to increase the student's skills thereby tapping the full potential of the students. The evaluation process of projects undertaken under Aanandam need to be based both on qualitative and quantitative methods. Thus mentors evaluating projects undertaken under Aanandam need to assess and evaluate projects of student groups so that students are made aware of which types of community services were useful or not. Evaluation of community service projects will help to impact the community in strategic ways.

Mentors or evaluators should base their evaluation by first looking for answers to the following questions: -

1. Did the participation of students in a given project lead to an increase in their interaction levels?
2. Was the project in which students engaged one of their choice?
3. Did working in the project reveal any hidden potential or talent or creativity in any/some students?
4. Did working on a project develop the ability of introspection among students for making their lives more socially engaging?
5. Did the service extended by the student groups actually help the target group?
6. What percentage of support did the target group experience?
7. Did the project move in the it was planned?
8. Did the project help in the way it was intended to?
9. On which steps did the project fall short?

The Community service projects undertaken by students should consistently pass through three important steps in the entire duration of the project. For this Aanandam day on any working day had been fixed. On this day students as well as Mentors will discuss their projects on the following 3 steps to evaluate.

Stage 1: Synopsis

This is the most vital stage for a future project that will be undertaken by student groups and will be mentored by their teachers. In this stage the students will required to:

1. Identify one or more local problems that need to be solved
2. Set goals which should be specifically divided in short and long term goals
3. They should discuss how they can change or solve the problem by identifying the cause of the problem.

Stage 2: Act

1. In this stage the students will chalk a baseline which will be created by making a project proposal, meeting minutes and incorporating suggestions of all participants
2. They will also consider the most practical an effective way to change the problem this can be done by breaking the broad long term goals in short and medium goals
3. Visualize an anticipate the outcome or result off the project to be undertaken
4. Consider what steps will bring about the desired change
5. What resources will be needed to solve the problems identified.

6. In this stage the students may require to design a questionnaire for the target groups regarding a specific problem
7. Before undertaking the project, the student groups need to interview the target groups or hold interactive discussions with different age groups, gender and social groups. This will help them to make clear cut customized goals.
8. Revise the short medium and long term goals if required
9. Determine specific steps that will bring about the desired change

Stage 3: Evaluate

Evaluate the extent to which the student group was able to achieve the short medium and long term goals

Compare the nature of the problems at the beginning and after a project reached its completion

Organise the information collected during the project and see how closely the specific goals were met a list of obstacles and problems faced by the student groups that made achieving the set goals or targets difficult to achieve or achieve partially satisfactorily also should be made how certain problems which were not anticipated earlier where resolved list other successful outcomes not figuring in the objectives but attained by the student groups in the course of the project.

Analyse if the success in achieving goals set earlier pertains to the problems identified earlier

Observations should be shared on Aanandam day each month to monitor contribution of each member and his or her potential or expertise for a certain job this will help in work distribution of the project.

In this stage the case studies of earlier projects undertaken on similar issues can also be discussed to compare the success rate. Important indicators to measure the success of a community service project would be Self-evaluation of student groups themselves

Number of people the student groups were able to reach. (For employment, health check-ups etc.)

Response of the target groups through feedback forms or personal interaction to record the opinion of people their views and experiences of the programme photos of before and after percentage of people who were not benefited.

Sharing the findings an observation will help the groups to recognise and identify problems or issues that prevented the progress of their projects sharing will also help to learn from mistakes and use successful ideas of other projects sharing will also help students to use their findings to make practical changes they had visualised

In this stage of evaluation, the mentors as well as students will be able to identify the factors that affected the achievement of the objectives. Such factors may be external or internal.

External factors: change in situation related to a problem (say poor rains affecting a project on plantation) or Supporting groups from the community withdrawing financial or infrastructural support. (pandemic, local pressures, politics etc.)

Internal factors: Key members leave the group or do not make the mandatory field trips, or devote enough time or resources. Project departs from the original plan.

All members not doing their tasks satisfactorily. Work done was satisfactory but not recorded well in project writing. The targets or objectives set were not realistic or appropriate. Project members could not work in unison.

Chapter 10

Aanandam: A Roadmap for the Future

With the progress of the time accompanied by the growth of the population, our civilisation is finding itself entrapped in the VUCA situation- where there is too much volatility, uncertainty, complexity, and ambiguity. To minimise its impact and to survive in this world our next generations needto be prepared. They should be empowered with velocity, unusual solutions, clarity, adaptability, and stability. Textbookish knowledge is justnot sufficient for making our youth resilient and robust to face the ups and downs of life. At least some part of the total time devoted to the routine type of education should be spent on community interactions and interaction with self.

The New National education policy 2020 envisions transformative changes in the present education system to make it more meaningful. Introduction of the new subject Aanandam is expected to bring such changes.

Outcomes of the Group Projects

1. Movement for literacy

The focus is on encouraging adolescent girls in tribal communities to go to school. Due to the heavy responsibilities of the household and stark poverty the girls in backward tribal communities are not sent to school, they sit at home doing household chores and taking care of their siblings. Their parents simply discourage them from going to school, whereas they have a great desire to study and go to school. The students will try to understand the realities of tribal life and will focus on the issues of adolescent girls. They will conduct a small survey to identify out-of-school girls. They would interact with the elders of the community. They would try to convince them about the importance of education.

This task can be a little challenging but the students will try to understand their dialects and use all their communication skills to make them understand how the education of the adolescent girls in the community can help in making their lives happier.

The group of students who take up this project will also help the girls in ameliorating their conditions by coordinating with the village administration, NGOs in the field, philanthropists, and political leaders. By doing this the students will use their communication skills, leadership skills, and other faculties in bringing the adolescent girls in the tribal community out of their homes and enrolling them into the school. This project can be continued further for the empowerment of adolescent girls by discussing with them the health-related issues: sanitation, hygiene, nutrition, and financial issues.

2. Taking care of Stray animals

The students can plan a project to take care of stray animals such as cows, dogs, etc.

They can involve the community to make them aware of the condition of the stray animals with the help of the community, they can feed them, they can take care of their health, and can help the injured birds and animals.

3. Plantation

A group of students can take up a project related to planting and converting a wasteland into a beautiful green area. The students will coordinate with local authorities and the community to procure the plants and plant them properly in the targeted area, they will learn how to take care of the plants, which fertilizers to be used, how the seeds are sown, and how different plants need different kinds of attention. This activity will contribute to the ecology of the area and will also make the students and the community happy.

A group of Students under the mentorship of a lecturer can take up a task to make a patch of barren land in the college campus, green. The purpose is to make the environs of the college campus look beautiful.

A green area acts as Oxyzone.

Now this work can be turned into four projects under Aanandam

Making the undulated land plain for the purpose of plantation.

Planting and maintenance of the trees

Arranging water for irrigating the plants-activate rainwater harvesting system, its maintenance, using water saving techniques like drip irrigation system.

Surveillance of the plants -using innovative and imaginative skills -

The mentor would guide the students. The groups for the project work can consist of a mix of students from different streams or it can be from the same stream-it is the discretion of the students and mentor teachers.

4. Organising blood donation camps and arranging the blood for the needy patients

This project will also be done by involving the community around the students to spread awareness about the importance of blood donation. They would coordinate with the blood banks, they would act as liaisons between the blood bank and the needy patients. For this, they can also think about some digital solutions. This activity is surely going to help the community and the needy people and in turn, will make the students happy and empathetic.

5. Improving the conditions of the Aanganwadis

The students can choose a village or slum as an area of the project If college so wishes it can decide upon the area after consultation with the students

Students will go to the site and will interact with the concerned persons for studying the Anganwadis. Then they will decide upon which Aanganwadis they would like to choose for the project work.

An Anganwadi caters to children up to 6 years and pregnant ladies and lactating mothers of deprived sections of society.

The task can be divided into a brief study of the community around the Anganwadi. The student will get familiar with the food habits, status of women, sources of livelihood, belief system, etc. of the community.

This brief study about the community will be an essential part of the project report.

An Anganwadi is run under Integrated Child Development Services.The scheme envisages taking care of the child before and after birth till six years of age.

The students can contribute to the proper implementation of the scheme, by encouraging the community to send their children to Anganwadi, by supervising the immunisation program and healthcare ofthe beneficiaries, by involving themselves in early childhood education that's imparted to 3-6yrs children. By contributing to improving Anganwadi building, and other articles that are necessary for the anganwadi. By contributing to the poshanvatika of the anganwadi. By coordinating with well-off people of the locality to support the anganwadi by providing clean drinking water, vessels, mats for children and other necessary equipment.

So a number of groups can take up different anganwadis for ameliorating and make them Model Anganwadis. The students will interact with the ICDS officials, the village head, ward members, NGO if any to make their project worthwhile.

6. **Women empowerment**

A group of students can take up projects on issues related to women empowerment

- ❖ Health Hygiene including menstrual hygiene and sanitation
- ❖ Nutrition
- ❖ Literacy-financial literacy, computer literacy, legal literacy etc.

Such projects can be taken up in a mohalla, slum, or a village ward. The projects related to women issues would certainly make the students gender sensitive and gender neutral. At the same time such projects would certainly go a long way in ameliorating the conditions of women in a community.

7. **Environment**

- Projects on water saving
- Projects on electricity saving
- Projects on fuel saving

- Projects on plantations
- Projects related to pollution control

or any other environmental related issues which the students want to take up. Such projects will expose the students to the problem of scarce natural resources viz water, electricity, fuel etc. In trying to solve the problem related to the scarcity of the resources the students may come out with very good ideas and innovations which would benefit the community. The projects related to pollution control like reducing the use of plastic etc. can result in discovery of some alternatives of the plastic. These projects can also be converted into startups.

CONCLUSION

Education cannot be limited to acquiring more and more information from textbooks and evaluating this accumulated information in term - end examinations. Such type of education is not making us connected with ourselves and the people around us. It doesn't teach us about making a healthy relationships with people and the environment around us. Mere accumulation of facts and figures cannot be defined as knowledge. It is necessary that the student should also understand about life. The processes of life can be understood only when the student is given the chance to interact with his own self and with the people around. After fulfilling the basic needs an individual want to satisfy his self-actualization need which can be fulfilled through use of creative and imaginative faculties. Only that education can be said to be holistic which allows the students to express his urge for creativity. There should be equal emphasis on experiencing the beauty and mystery of Nature. To make education joyful experience there should be a subject where the students can interact with the community and the nature using their faculties of kindness, empathy, creativity and imagination. Then only the student will enjoy learning and will assimilate it for living a joyful life.

To conclude, few lines from Rabindranath Tagore

"Aanondo Loke mongola Loke birajo shotto shundoro"

O Beautiful Truth grace the world of happiness and benevolence.

Indian philosophy revolves around Satyam Shivam Sundaram -Truth is beautiful and benevolent-

Aanandam emphasizes Harmony, it makes the students enjoy the music of Nature and understand the harmony in the ecosystem. It makes them inquisitive. They question and enjoy the journey of discovering and unfolding the truth. They interact with the community and understand the underlying interdependence. They become empathetic. Aanandam course through its contents tries to make the student a part of the whole-makes them realize their necessity to sustain the system.

APPENDIX

Implementation of Aanandam in Higher and Technical Education in Rajasthan

The idea of Aanandam was conceived by the author of the book when she was Secretary Higher and Technical Education Department in Government of Rajasthan. Meetings with Vice Chancellors of the Universities and Good NGOs were held. The task force comprising experienced educationists and NGOs deliberated over the issue of how to make Aanandam course an integral part of the curriculum. After much deliberations Aanandam has been accepted as a graded compulsory subject for all technical and non-technical courses in Higher and Technical education in Rajasthan. The Academic Councils of many Universities accepted Aanandam as a compulsory graded subject. The Directorate of Polytechnic Institutes also incorporated Aanandam as a graded subject for all diploma courses. Though the progress of this new subject suffered during almost two years long lockdown of Pandemic, but wherever there is enthusiastic faculty, it has shown good results. Some private universities like Apex University, Shree Keshwanand Institute of Technology, Nims University are also doing good community service projects under Aanandam. Some examples are shared in this book.

Implementation of Aanandam in Ram Chandra Khaitan Government Polytechnic Institute in Jaipur, Rajasthan

For implementing Aanandam in a Polytechnic institute in Rajasthan the following steps were taken –

1. **Appointment of Aanandam Nodal Officer**

   To monitor the course at the Institutional level, a passionate faculty member was to be entrusted with the task of implementation of Aanandam. A Nodal officer was appointed and entrusted with the responsibility of proper execution of Aanandam activities in the institute.

2. All the faculty members are to act as Group Project mentors for their respective classes. The Principal of the institute will from time to time supervise the activities being done under Aanandam.

3. **Student group formation**

   The students will themselves decide their groups and the activities they want to take up as group projects. The records of the groups and their respective project works are to be maintained at the level of the class. The group size may vary between 10-15 students depending on the nature of the project work.

4. **Activities by students:**

   Under Aanandam the students will undertake the following two kinds of activities

(i) Individual acts of goodness to be recorded daily:

Every student, will perform a good act with the intention to help of people or nature. This individual act of goodness will be recorded in the Aanandam Diary. Entry in the Aanandam Diary should be on daily basis

(ii) Group Community Project

Each student group will undertake a project towards the welfare of the community. Each and every student will actively participate

A synopsis has to be submitted by the group to their mentor about the work to be undertaken. Finally, the project report will be submitted to the mentor clearly explaining the beneficiaries, procedures and outcomes of the project.

Students can take financial support through NGOs, community schemes, Govt. Schemes etc., if possible.

5. Aanandam Period Allocation:

The institute should devote half an hour to one hour per week for the interaction of students with their mentors.

6. Aanandam Day Celebration:

To motivate and support the students 'Aanandam Day' should be celebrated. On 'Aanandam Day' the student groups will discuss the progress of their project works. A renowned social personality could be invited for a motivational speech.

The students can present their project work by displaying charts or video clips. Aanandam day could be celebrated per month or per semester.

7. Project Assessment Committee (PAC):

To evaluate and give recognition to efforts of students in their project, at institute level, a project assessment committee has been constituted comprising the followings as PAC members: Principal / Principal Nominee A social representative, Nodal Officer and 2 to 5 Mentors.

8. **Awarding the best 'Aanandam Project':**

As decided by PAC, 1st and 2nd best projects should be awarded by the institute. The award may be given on Aanandam day, Republic Day or on Independence Day celebration.

If the projects really have very good impact on society, they may be presented at the government level for recognition.

The institute undertook the following projects

1. **Educating children in a slum area**

Location: Slum area, Near Mansarovar metro station, Jaipur (Raj.)

Purpose: To provide primary education to the children residing in slum areas.

Methodology: The students selected the area, spoke to children's parents about the importance of education, and sought permission from them. The students also provided the children food and thereafter imparted some basic education.

Activities:

The students taught the children about

- The alphabets,
- Writing small words and numbers,
- Basic addition and subtraction,
- Good habits,
- About our nation, national flag and national anthem and
- Benefits of education.

Outcomes:

The children were able to

- Write and read Hindi and English alphabets,
- Write and read their names
- Write and read Numbers
- Write tables
- Adopt some good habits
- Sing national anthem

POCO

POCO

POCO

POCO

2. Caring and Feeding of Animals and Birds

Location: Cowsheds, local area streets, Jaipur (Raj.)

Purpose: To take care and feed the animals and birds.

Methodology: The students planned to take care and feed the animals and birds by devoting time and providing food/stuff/grains. They also urged other people to help the birds/animals and feed them, whenever possible.

Activities:

The students did the following activities

- Feeding birds/animals with grains and fodder.
- Filling water feeder pots whenever/wherever possible
- Taking care of birds/animals
- Helping the injured birds/animals
- Spreading awareness among the local people for taking care of birds/animals
- The street animals/birds have been taken care of.
- Food for street animals/birds was provided.
- The students were boosted ethically.
- Parents and people around felt proud of the good gestures of the students and the education system.
- This act set an example for others around to practice similar acts.

REDMI NOTE 9 PRO MAX
AI QUAD CAMERA

3. **Plantation**

Location: College campus, local area gardens and communities, Jaipur (Raj.)

Purpose: To grow useful plant species at different sites.

Methodology: The students selected areas where plantation was needed. Discussed with a mentor for the plants needed at specific sites, took the help of teachers and other supporting people to manage/purchase the plants. Planted saplings at different sites and took care of plants thereafter by fertilizing and watering plants.

Activities:

The students did the following activities

- Selected the location for the plantation.
- Manage the plants with help of teachers and other supporting people.
- Plantation was done
- Used fertilisers for the healthy growth of plants
- Watering and caring for the plants from time to time.
- Motivated society to conserve the environment.

Outcomes:

- Clean and green area was developed.
- Beautification of the College campus/park was done through plantation.
- Other people were also motivated by the plantation activity by students.
- Natural activities of birds increased at plantation zones.
- The students became aware and also spread awareness for environment conservation.

आर्किटेक्चर विभाग

4. Participation in blood donation camps

Location: Blood banks, local community areas Jaipur (Raj.)

Purpose: To provide blood to the needy people and to spread awareness for blood donation.

Methodology: Donating blood at blood banks and making people aware about the importance of blood donation.

Activities:

The students did the following activities

- Donated blood in the blood bank (those who were 18+).
- Contributed voluntarily for gathering people for blood donation.
- Made people aware of the importance of blood donation in their local areas.
- local campaigning by telling the health benefits of blood donation.

Outcomes:

- The activity supported the blood donor organisations.
- Increased the chances of blood availability to needy people.
- Helped to remove the myths in the society regarding blood donation.
- Such volunteer outreach activities made the students confident and ethically strong.

Up-gradation of a cycle to e-cycle

Purpose: To upgrade a cycle to an environment-friendly and affordable alternative of e-cycle for the use of street vendors.

The students were moved by the plight of „thelawalas" (street vendors) and thought of inventing some engineering solution to help them.

Students designed a cycle with a specific tyre size keeping in view the battery and the load to be carried keeping in view factors like voltage, temperature, current using conditions and transportation requirements. A rechargeable battery pack has was used and fixed in the cycle to make it power driven. Different measures were taken into consideration while designing the frame.

Outcomes/Results

- E- Cycle was successfully prepared and trails of the prototype e-cycle was also undertaken
- The proposed e-cycle was environment friendly and consumes less electrical energy as compared to prevailing e-bikes.
- Can be used by any age group for cycling and exercise
- The e-cycle can be used to carry and move loads thereby lessening the burden of the vendors and conserving their energy
- The proposed e-cycle especially could be an affordable option for the aged people of poor section of the society.

Highlights of upgraded e-cycle:

- Approximate cost is 12000/-
- Equipped with indicators.

- Used power brakes to control speed.
- Travelling 20-25 km is single charge.
- Speed 30 km/hour.
- No need for registration and licence.
- Eco-friendly.

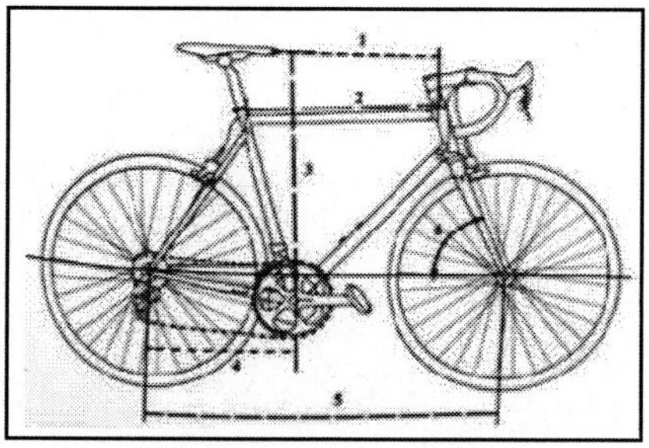
Frame designing for e-cycle

Actual designed e-cycle

Maintenance of rainwater harvesting systems in college premises

Purpose: To maintain the rain water harvesting system in order to meet the water requirements in the premises.

Prospective Students: Civil engineering students can undertake such kinds of projects.

Methodology: Since Rainwater harvesting structures are used to conserve and send rainwater into the ground at a particular depth so that this water further recharges the underlying water table, the following key factors need to be kept in mind

- For proper functioning of the water harvesting system regular maintenance is required so the outer part of the existing chambers should be repaired.
- The water harvesting chambers should be made deeper
- Chambers and pipes connected to harvesting tanks should be checked and maintained on regular basis
- The filtering material (coarse aggregate and sand) should be washed/ changed frequently.

Proposed Outcomes/Results:

- This project would help to preserve more pure water.
- As a result of rain water harvesting the level of the water table will come rise.
- In the nearby areas the water demand would be met locally.
- This water can be used for some or farming and other supporting activities.
- Tube-wells could be planned near the harvesting system
- Rain water is pure and of good quality so the soil quality of nearby areas would be improved.

Water harvesting chambers in the college premises

Present outside and inside conditions of harvesting chambers

Title: Developing a medicinal plants zone in college campus

Methodology/ procedures adopted: The importance of medical plants in routine life is increasing, so it was planned to develop a small area where some medicinal plants are available for use by students. Govt. Ramchandra Khaitan Polytechnic College, Jaipur teachers helped the students in developing the zone. On plantation day the program 'Haritotsav' was celebrated and many plants were planted at different sites of the college. For the safety of plants tree guards were used.

Outcomes / Results:

- A medicinal plant zone has been developed in the college campus.
- Green area has increased in the college campus.
- Contributed in the beautification of the college campus.
- College staff and students can now take advantage of the medicinal plant in the campus itself.

Installing drip system for watering the plants

Purpose: To install a drip system to supply water to the plants.

Prospective Students: Students of all branches can take on such kinds of projects.

Methodology/procedures adopted: In Rajasthan, there has always been crises of water even for drinking purposes; hence, it becomes s challenging to water the plants. Supplying water through a drip system to each plant location seems a plausible and effective solution, therefore it was planned to install the drip system in the developed park and green zones. For this the pipes, nozzle, valve and other required items have been purchased/arranged from the market and resource persons and with the help of staff, students and technicians of college, the drip system has been installed. This activity was undertaken in Govt. Ramchandra Khaitan Polytechnic College, Jaipur and Govt. Polytechnic College, Udaipur under the supervision of faculty in mechanical engineering branch.

Outcomes/Results:

- Drip systems for watering the plants has been installed in different locations of college campus.
- The water is now automatically supplied to all the plants with a single point valve control.
- This drip system becomes more significant in the summer season.
- By the drip system, water is supplied slowly and directly to the root into the soil and hence there is no wastage of water in this system.

Placing the drip system for watering the plants

Title: Development of GSM (SMS) based automated drip water supply to plants (Undertaken example)

Purpose: To develop GSM (Global System of Mobile) based automated motor drip water supply to plants via detecting the moisture level.

Prospective Students: Electronics, civil and computer engineering branch students.

Methodology/ procedures adopted: In the present world scenario, there is a need to conserve the environment and water simultaneously. Especially in our Rajasthan state, there is a rigorous need of conserving greenery and watering the plants in a frugal way without wastage. Keeping this in mind, the students group decided to develop a water-supplying system with GSM communication control. This project was undertaken by the Govt. Ramchandra Khaitan Polytechnic College, Jaipur.

The required equipment/devices are as depicted in the figure below –

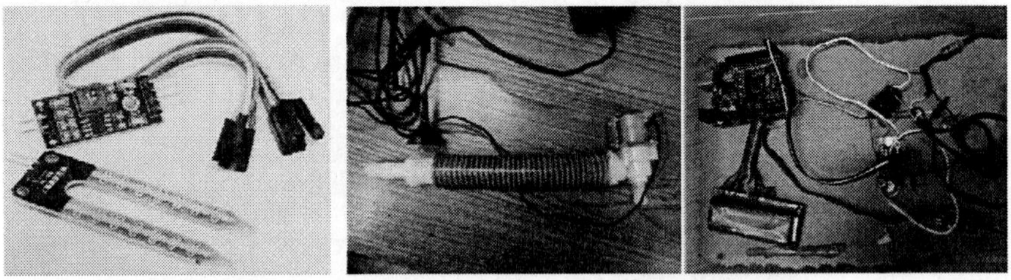

Moisture detection sensor, connector with value and relay control, and LCD display with control and communication devices

Project demonstrated by the students and won the prize (prize was given by Rajasthan Environment and Energy Conservation Center.)

Functioning of SMS based drip system:

When soil is dry the user receives an SMS on mobile as -

Soil moisture is low ..... Reply to ON pump (a message code is used for that pump)

Tp switch off the system the user receives an SMS on mobile as –

Soil moisture is high .... Reply to OFF pump (a message code is used for that pump)

Outcomes/Results

- In the present hectic lifestyle, if someone forgets to water the plant/lawn, there is no need to worry. The water supply can be switched on by mobile from the location from wherever you are.
- The drip of the sprinkler can be positioned in such a way to efficiently supply the water at the desired place where it is needed.
- The dripping system can be made underground to hide the hoses stretches around the lawn.
- One can switch off the water supply when the water requirements are completed by detecting the moisture level signal in a mobile sent by the sensor.
- This water supply technique saves water as it reduces the water wastage due to overwatering and evaporation in comparison to conventional watering methods.

„Aanandam" will definitely change the thought of youth in the positive direction.

Dr. Pramod Sain
Aanandam Nodal Officer,
Govt. Ramchandra Khaitan
Polytechnic College, Jaipur
(Raj.)

It was really a great experience while implementing the Aanandam course first time in the Govt. Ramchandra Khaitan Polytechnic College, Jaipur. With the cooperation of college faculty, the course was strictly implemented and followed in the college. With different activities under Aanandam, the helping, and problem-solving attitude is being developed in the students.

In the present scenario, there is a big focus to prepare skilled person for different industrial sectors, however, the un-employability is still a very big issue in our country. The reason behind this is a lack of idea, confidence, and ethics. There is a need to orient education in such a way that every skilled person could be a source of employment and this is only possible when the prospective youths connect with the real need and problems of the community. This interaction during education will definitely give a large number of ideas and instill confidence and ethics among the students.

I personally felt that Aanandam course provides the chance to learn ideas and confidence. Engagement in the daily act of goodness makesthe students ethically rich and sensible for the problems around them. In addition, the community project provides different circumstances and challenges to face which is important for building confidence. Through this course, the students are connecting with society, knowing the needs, demands and problems of society. This awareness would give them ideas for start– up projects after their academic life and increase their chances of employability.

Aanandam In Apex University, Rajasthan
Social Outreach, Discipline & Extra-Curricular Activities

1. In Apex University, Social Outreach, Discipline & Extra-Curricular Activities (SODECA) has been introduced in all courses and in each semester from the 2022 batch onwards. In order to implement this subject, the following actions have been initiated:-

(a) A presentation on 'SODECA' covering all relevant aspects including the assessment scheme has been conducted for all faculty members at all Campuses.

(b) Department-wise **'Aanandam Nodal Officer'** (ANO) has been nominated.

(c) A meeting of ANOs has been conducted. Individual and group activities have been discussed. The Excel sheet prepared for the Evaluation of SODECA and other activities (Sports, NCC, NSS, Technoagaz, and Volunteer) has been explained. A copy of the same is attached as an annexure.

(d) Introductory sessions of "SODECA" for all Departments have been conducted. All ANOs have planned group activities and projected resources support required from the University.

(e) CoE has finalized the code for the subject. The same has been incorporated into the teaching and exam schemes of all disciplines. 1 credit/50 marks have been assigned for the subject in each semester.

2. **Group Activities.**

As a part of group activities, students of Commerce & Management department visited Aashraya Care Home, an Orphanage House located in Brijalpura, Mansaronvar, Jaipur. This house accommodates 32 girl children age ranging 5-18 years. In this visit, 42 students of Apex participated. They contributed and donated groceries, clothes, food items, stationery, utensils, plants, etc. They have also conducted a small cultural programme to entertain the children staying in the Orphanage House. A few photographs of the activity are shown below:-

3. **Students Individual Daily Acts Diaries**:

Students have started writing diaries and good acts are being mentioned. Some examples with one beautiful cover page of the diary are given below:-

4. **Futuristic Plans.** As a part of group activities of SODECA, students are planning to visit Old Age Homes, Cancer Hospital, Cow Shelter, etc. Tree plantation, Shramdaan, motivational talks, etc havealso been planned in forthcoming months.

Nims University Rajasthan, Jaipur conducting 14 Social Champions in the periphery region of the university (Around 20kms) under the umbrella of AANANDAM

Various social welfare activities are being organized by Nims University Rajasthan, Jaipur under AANANDAM

1- Nirogi Manush

- Health Awareness Camps in Villages
- Cancer Awareness
- Heart Disease & Life-style Diseases Awareness
- Diabetes Awareness
- STD Awareness
- Drug Addiction Awareness
- Dental Health Awareness

2. Waste Disposal Plan

- Bio-Waste Management
- Bio-waste Awareness
- Bio-waste Bins
- Bio-Waste STP

सफाई कर दिया स्वच्छता का संदेश, जगाई ज्ञान की अलख

जयपुर, समाचार जगत न्यूज। दिल्ली रोड स्थित निम्स

3. **Aao Khele**

- Sports Development Program
- Sports training (Kabbadi & KhoKho) in Villages
- Sports Awareness

4. **Saathi Haath Badhana**

- Program for Handicapped
- Prosthetic Limbs Donation
- Wheel-chair Donation
- Handicapped Rehabilitation Training with Prosthesis
- Plant for Prosthetic Implants for handicapped

5. **Swasthya Gyan Yojana**

- First Aid Skills Development
- Basic Life Support Skills Certification
- First Aids skill Certifications

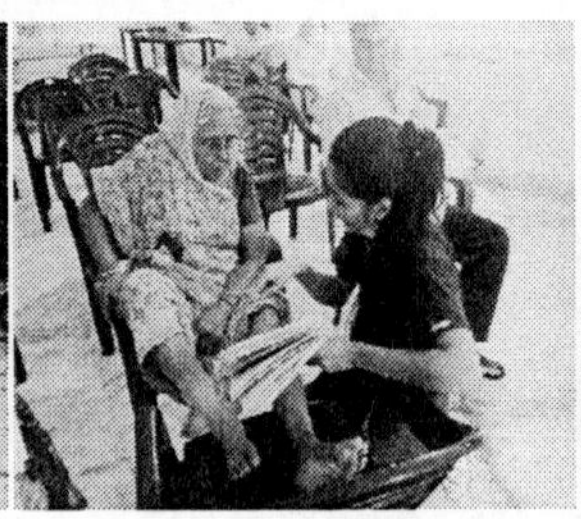

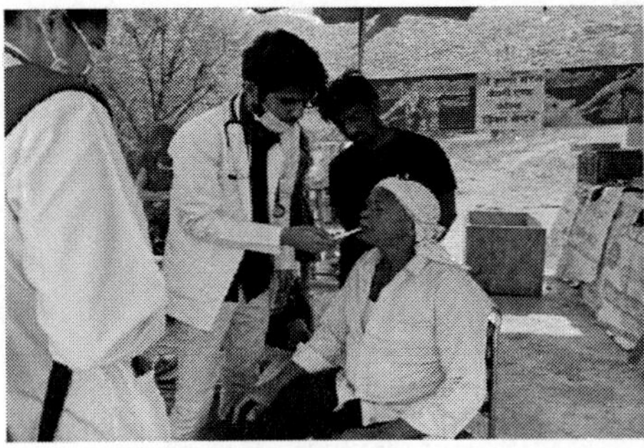

6. **Meri Dawa Teri Dawa**

- Unused Medicines Program
- Medicines un-used by patients getting discharged to be used for poor needy patients

7. **Samaj Nasha Mukti Manch**

- Say No to Drugs, Yes to Sports Program
- Making Kabaddi Team of former Addicts to participate in sports events
- Addiction Awareness
- Free De-addiction facility
- Lifestyle re-structuring program for former addicts

8. **Anashrya Antodaya**

- Orphan Personality/Social Development Program
- Free Education
- Free Clothing, books and other needs
- Personality Development Workshops

- Vocational Skill Development Program
- Scholarships for School/College Education

9. Widow Education Donation

- Widow Education Campaign
- Widow Literacy
- Vocational Skill Endowment (Widow/Widow's Children)
- Widow Job Placement
- Widow's Child Scholarship
- Widow's Child Employment

REFERENCES

1. AS Altekar; Education in Ancient India
2. AV Krishnarao; The Relevance Of Gandhiji's Sarvodaya, Education and Vedanta Philosophy In Modern Era
3. Charles Vogl; The Art of Community: Seven Principles of Belonging
4. Cohn, Diana; Gans, Ruth; Miller, Bob; Selman, Ruth; and Miller, Ron (1990). "Parallel Paths: A Conversation Among Montessori and Waldorf Educators" Holistic Education Review 3:4.
5. Emerson, Ralph Waldo (1965). "Education" and "Self-Reliance." Selected Writings. Edited by William H. Gilman. New York: New American Library.
6. HH Dalai Lama and Howard C. Cutler; The Art Of Happiness In A Troubled World
7. Kessler, Rachael (2000) The Soul of Education: Helping Students Find Connection, Compassion and Character at School. Alexandria, VA: ASCD.
8. Krishnamurti, J. (1975). The First and Last Freedom. San Francisco: Harper.
9. Miller, Ron (1990). What Are Schools For? Holistic Education in American Culture. Brandon, VT: Holistic Education Press.
10. Miller, Ron (2000). "Partial Vision in Alternative Education," in Caring for New Life: Essays on Holistic Education. Brandon, VT: Foundation for Educational Renewal.
11. MK Gandhi; India Of My Dreams
12. Osho World; Liberation Through Education - Osho on Education
13. Packer, Toni (2002). The Wonder of Presence and the Way of

Meditative Inquiry. Boston: Shambhala.

14. Palmer, Parker (1993). To Know as We Are Known: Education as a Spiritual Journey. San Francisco: Harper.
15. Rabindranath Tagore's Educational Ideas and Experiments Scottish Centre of Tagore Studies
16. Radha Kumud Mookerji; Ancient Indian Education Brahmanical andBuddhist
17. RC Majumdar; Ancient India
18. RC Majumdar; The History and Culture Of the Indian People, Bhartiya Vidya Bhawan Series
19. R Sarkar; Swami Vivekananda's Idea and Philosophy of Education; A Way Out To Promote Imperishable Development Of The Nation – Scholar's Impact Quarterly Research General (July - September 2015)
20. The Golden Future Education Osho International
21. Tolle, Eckhart (1999). The Power of Now: A Guide to Spiritual Enlightenment. Novato, CA: New World Library.